DOUBLE CLONE

BY MELANIE JOYCE

ILLUSTRATED BY SI CLARK

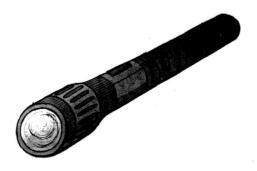

Titles in Full Flight Heroes & Heroines

Who Are You?	David Orme
3Dee	Danny Pearson
Doom Clone	Melanie Joyce
Too Risky!	Alison Hawes
Wanda Darkstar	Jane A C West
Galactic Games: Sci-Fi Spy Guy	Roger Hurn
Robot Eyes	Jillian Powell
Charlie's Tin	Lynda Gore
Run For Your Life	Jonny Zucker
Changing Rooms	Melanie Joyce

Badger Publishing Limited
Oldmedow Road, Hardwick Industrial Estate,
King's Lynn PE30 4JJ
Telephone: 01438 791037
www.badgerlearning.co.uk

2 4 6 8 10 9 7 5 3

Doom Clone ISBN 978 1 84926 480 8

First edition © 2011
This second edition © 2014

Text © Melanie Joyce 2011
Complete work © Badger Publishing Limited 2011

All rights reserved. No part of this publication may be reproduced, stored in any form or by any means mechanical, electronic, recording or otherwise without the prior permission of the publisher.

The right of Melanie Joyce to be identified as author of this Work has been asserted by her in accordance with the Copyright, Designs and Patents Act 1988.

Badger Publishing would like to thank Jonny Zucker for his help in putting this series together.

Publisher: David Jamieson
Senior Editor: Danny Pearson
Design: Fiona Grant
Illustration: Si Clark

CONTENTS

CHAPTER 1	**The Journey**	PAGE 5
CHAPTER 2	**Voices**	PAGE 10
CHAPTER 3	**The Clones**	PAGE 14
CHAPTER 4	**Shadows**	PAGE 18
CHAPTER 5	**Lift Off**	PAGE 23
UFOs		PAGE 30
QUESTIONS		PAGE 32

New words:

rattled	distress
struggled	quarry
clone	drained
stumbled	repeated

Main characters:

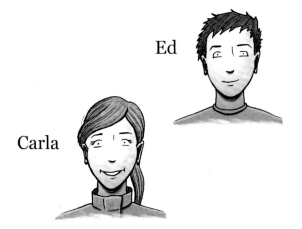

Ed

Carla

Dad

CHAPTER 1
The Journey

Ed couldn't wait to go camping.
His sister, Carla, wasn't so keen.

Dad had driven for hours. Finally, they had reached the mountain.

The sun was setting.

"Is the campsite far?" said Ed.

"Not too far, I hope," replied Dad. "It's getting dark."

Suddenly, a voice spoke. It was the Sat Nav. "Take the next left," it said.

Dad was puzzled. "I don't remember a turning here," he said.

"Turn left," repeated the voice.

The Sat Nav screen flashed on and off. The voice repeated the message.

Dad slowed the car. On the left was a narrow track. It led into the darkness.

"Turn left," said the Sat Nav.

Ed had a strange feeling. "I'm sure this isn't right," he said.

Dad drove the car down the track.
It was steep and rocky. The old car
rattled and shook.

The track led to an open space. It was dry and stony. Dust drifted in the beam of the headlights.

"Where are we?" said Carla.

"Not at the campsite," replied Dad.

He switched the car engine off.
It was pitch black. Ed reached into the back seat. He grabbed a torch.

"It's like a quarry," he said. "Why would the Sat Nav lead us here?"

"It must be faulty," replied Dad.

He reached for his phone. There was no signal. "I can't get GPS," he said. "We'll just have to camp here tonight."

Ed looked into the silent dark.
This place gave him the creeps.

CHAPTER 2
Voices

It was the dead of night. Dad and Carla were asleep. Ed was wide awake.

He sensed danger. But he didn't know why. It was as if they weren't alone.

"I'm going to get the distress flare," he said. "I've got a bad feeling about this place."

It was dark outside. Ed opened the car boot. He reached for a large flare.
Then he heard a voice.

It sounded like the Sat Nav.

It was coming from the darkness.

The voice was clear.

"Go straight ahead," it said. What was going on?

Ed put the flare back in the car.

He walked towards the voice.
"Hello?" he called. There was no reply.

A shape moved in the darkness.

Something grabbed Ed's arm. It was very strong. He waved his torch in panic.

The light fell on a creature. It had scales. Its eyes glowed red.

What was it?

The thing hissed at Ed.

He struggled to escape. The torch beam fell on another figure.

It hissed at the light, too.

But the second figure wasn't like the creature.

Ed's eyes grew wide with horror. It was an exact copy of him.

CHAPTER 3
The Clones

Carla woke suddenly. Something was wrong. She could sense it. Ed's sleeping bag was empty. Carla grabbed her torch.

She crept outside. Suddenly, someone called her.

"Come here," said a voice.

It was Ed. He was calling to her.

Without thinking, Carla stumbled forward.

A shape moved nearby.

"Is that you, Ed?" said Carla.

But there was silence.

Something shifted to her right. Carla spun round. Ed was standing there. He was staring at her. His eyes glowed red.

Carla felt a claw grip her arm. Then everything went black.

Carla woke in a strange room.

Dull lights went on and off. Her head ached.

Behind her, something moved.

It was Ed.

A rush of fear swept over Carla.

"It's OK," whispered Ed. "That wasn't me outside. It was an alien. There are two of them. They have cloned us. I think this is their spaceship."

"What do they want?" said Carla.

"I don't know," replied Ed. "But they don't like bright light. My torch light hurt their eyes."

Ed looked at Carla.

"We've got to get to Dad," he said. "He's in danger."

CHAPTER 4
Shadows

Dad opened his eyes. He clicked his torch on. He looked at his watch. It was 4.00 am.

Outside, he heard footsteps.

They were coming closer.

"Is that you, Ed? Carla?"

The footsteps stopped. Two shadows stood by the tent.

"Help us, Dad. Please, help us," they said.

Dad lay the torch on the floor. He flung the tent flap open.

"What's the matter?" he said.

Outside, the clones stared blankly.

"Help us," they repeated.

Dad was worried. Something was wrong. He scrambled out of the tent. The clones moved towards him.

On the spaceship, Ed looked for a way to escape. Shiny discs lined the walls.

He touched one. The dull lights went out. Ed touched another. There was a deep rumble.

"It sounds like an engine," said Carla. "Hurry!"

Ed touched another disc. Finally, a door slid open.

Carla and Ed could see Dad. The aliens were moving towards him.

"They're going to clone Dad," said Carla.

She tried to shout. Nothing came out.

"It's like they've drained us," she whispered.

Her limbs felt like lead.

Ed reached into his pocket.

There was a signal on his phone.

Ed called Dad's number. He saw his father reach into the tent. Dad grabbed the torch. He found his phone.
The clones stepped back.

"Dad," croaked Ed. "Run."

Suddenly, the line went dead.

CHAPTER 5
Lift Off

Dad looked up at the clones.
He thought they were Carla and Ed.

"Are you two playing tricks?" he said.

Suddenly, two figures stumbled from the dark.

"Dad. Run!" said a familiar voice.
The two figures came closer.

Dad couldn't believe his eyes.
They looked exactly like Carla and Ed.

Dad looked at the clones. He looked at the figures. He didn't know which was which.

Then, the female clone spoke.

"This is why we woke you, Dad," she said. "They are aliens. The signal from their ship drew us here. It is a trap. They have cloned us. They need your life force to survive."

"So that's what they want," whispered Ed to Carla. "We've got to stop them."

He stepped forward.

"Keep back," said Dad.
He held his hand out.

The clones smiled. They moved closer.
One raised a hand behind Dad's head.

"No!" cried Carla.

But there was no time. Suddenly, there was a hissing sound. The male clone leapt. He grabbed Dad. Carla ran to help him.

"No!" cried Ed.

The female clone dived onto Carla. She groaned in pain. Then Dad began to scream.

The aliens had changed form.
They made strange, gurgling noises.

The male opened his huge jaws.

"Absorb them," he said.

The female raised her head.

Ed was desperate. He staggered to the car. The flare was still there.

He grabbed it.

Behind him, the aliens were about to strike.

Ed held up the flare.

"Leave them alone!" he shouted.

He pulled the tab. The flare burst into light. It lit up the night.

The aliens screamed. The light hurt their eyes. They ran away into the darkness.

There was a terrible thundering. Suddenly, the spaceship ripped across out of the dark. It shot into the sky and was gone.

A heavy silence fell.

"Did that really happen?" whispered Dad.

"Yes, it really did," said Ed. "But I don't think they will be back."

He looked up at the mountain.
The rising sun spilled over the top.

"I told you camping was a bad idea," said Carla.

Dad and Ed agreed.

It was time to go home.

UFOs

UFO means Unidentified Flying Object.

Since ancient times, people have reported seeing UFOs.

In many cultures there are legends about people who come from the stars.

Evidence shows that most UFO reports are incorrect. People mistake bright stars, planets, or even aircraft for UFOs.

There have been many legends and theories about UFOs.
However, there is no absolute proof that they do exist.

Some sightings cannot be explained.

1896 – THE AMERICAN MIDWEST

Thousands of people saw a cigar-shaped object flying through the sky.
It was seen years before the first plane flight.

1952 – WASHINGTON AIRPORT

Air traffic controllers detected several moving objects on their radar.
They could not be identified. The air force launched fighter planes.
They could not find the objects.
No explanation has ever been found.

QUESTIONS

- *What gives directions in the car?*
- *Where does the narrow track lead to?*
- *What do the aliens do to Carla and Ed?*
- *At what time does Dad wake up?*
- *What makes the aliens hiss?*
- *Why won't the aliens come back?*